BV4909 .T4413 1974

On Suffering

Pierre Teilhard de Chardin

On Suffering

Harper & Row, Publishers
New York, Evanston, San Francisco, London

Sur la Souffrance was first published in 1974 by Editions du Seuil.

© Editions du Seuil, 1974

ON SUFFERING © in the English translation of extracts from the essay 'La Grande Monade' in *Ecrits du Temps de la Guerre*, the letter to Edouard Le Roy of 24 January 1927, the letter to Madame Henry Cosme of 9 May 1944, and the preface to Marguerite-Marie Teilhard de Chardin's *L'Energie Spirituelle de la Souffrance*, William Collins Sons & Co. Ltd, London, 1975.

The other extracts reproduced here are taken from books copyrighted as follows: *Le Milieu Divin* or *The Divine Milieu*, © in the English translation William Collins Sons & Co. Ltd, London, and Harper & Brothers, New York, 1960; *The Making of a Mind*, © in the English translation by William Collins Sons & Co. Ltd, London, and Harper & Row, New York, 1965; *Letters to Two Friends, 1926-1952*, Copyright © 1968 by The New American Library, Inc.; *Science and Christ*, © in the English translation William Collins Sons & Co. Ltd, London, and Harper & Row, Publishers, Inc., New York, 1968; *Writings in Time of War*, © in the English translation William Collins Sons & Co. Ltd, London, and Harper & Row, Publishers, Inc., New York, 1968; *Human Energy*, English translation © 1969 William Collins Sons & Co. Ltd, London; *Letters to Léontine Zanta*, © in the English translation William Collins Sons & Co. Ltd, London, and Harper & Row, Publishers, Inc., New York, 1969. The original French editions of *Le Milieu Divin*, *Science and Christ* and *Human Energy* were published by Editions du Seuil, of *The Making of a Mind*, *Letters to Two Friends, 1926-1952* and *Writings in Time of War* by Editions Bernard Grasset, and of *Letters to Léontine Zanta* by Desclée de Brouwer.

All rights reserved. Printed in Great Britain.
For information address Harper & Row, Publishers, Inc.,
10 East 53rd Street, New York, N.Y. 10022.
FIRST U.S. EDITION
ISBN 0 06 068211 6
Library of Congress Catalog Card Number: 75-18606

The extracts reproduced in this book are from the following translations:

Writings in Time of War (Collins, London, and Harper & Row, New York, 1968);

The Making of a Mind (Collins, London, and Harper & Row, New York, 1965);

Letters to Léontine Zanta (Collins, London, and Harper & Row, New York, 1969);

Science and Christ (Collins, London, and Harper & Row, New York, 1968);

Letters to Two Friends, 1926–1952 (The New American Library, New York, 1968, Rapp & Whiting, London, 1970, and Fontana, London, 1972);

Le Milieu Divin (Collins, London, 1960, and Fontana, London, 1964), published in the USA as *The Divine Milieu* (Harper & Brothers, New York, 1960);

Human Energy (Collins, London, 1969, and Harcourt Brace Jovanovich, New York, 1971).

Also included are new translations from the following French sources:

Ecrits du Temps de la Guerre (Editions Bernard Grasset, Paris, 1965);

Preface to *L'Energie Spirituelle de la Souffrance* by Marguerite-Marie Teilhard de Chardin (Editions du Seuil, Paris, 1951);
and from unpublished letters of Pierre Teilhard de Chardin to Edouard Le Roy and Madame Henry Cosme.

In an organism as vast as the universe any amount of goodwill and countless resources remain unused, and a host of failures is the price that has to be paid for a few successes. The obscure, the useless, the failures, should take joy in the superiority of the others whose triumph they lend support to or pay for. All this is indeed hard. The world, and subjection to the world, and the duty of serving the world, are hard to bear, like a cross; and it was *to force us to believe this* that Christ wished, overlooking all the highways of the earth, to rise up in the form of the Crucifix, the symbol in which every man could recognize his own true image.

We should like to be able to doubt

this, to hope that suffering and wickedness are transitory conditions of life, to be eliminated some day by science and civilization; but we must be more realistic and have the courage to look existence in the face. The more subtle and complex mankind becomes, the more numerous the chances of disorder and the greater their gravity; for one cannot build up a mountain without digging a great pit, and every energy has equal power for good and for evil. Everything that *becomes* suffers or sins. The truth about our position in this world is that *in it we are on a cross*.

Now, Christ did not wish his distressful figure to be no more than a warning permanently dominating the world. On Calvary he is still, and primarily, *the centre* on which all earthly sufferings *converge* and in which they are all *assuaged*. We have very little evidence about the way our Lord *tests* his mystical body, in order to take delight in it, but we can get some idea of how he can gather to himself its sufferings; and the only way, even, we can appreciate the immensity of his agony is to see in it an anguish that reflects every anguish ever experienced, *a 'cosmic' suffering*. During his Passion, Christ felt that he bore upon his soul, alone and battered, the weight of all human sorrows – in a fantastic synthesis no words can express. All these he took to himself, and all these he suffered.

Further, by admitting them into the domain of his consciousness, he transfigured them. Without Christ, suffering and sin would be the earth's 'slagheap'. The waste-products of the world's activities would pile up into a mountain of laborious effort, efforts that failed, efforts that had been 'suppressed'. Through the virtue of the cross this great mass of debris has become a store of treasure: man has understood that the most effective means of progress is to make use of suffering, ghastly and revolting though it be.

The Christian experiences suffering just as other men do. As others, so must he do his best to lessen and alleviate it, not only by humble prayer but also through the efforts of an industrious and self-confident science; but when the time comes when suffering is inevitable, then he puts it to good use. There is a wonderful compensation by which physical evil, if humbly accepted, conquers moral evil. In accordance with definable psychological laws, it purifies the soul, spurs it on and detaches it. Finally, acting as a sacrament acts, it effects a mysterious union between the faithful soul and the suffering Christ.

If it is undertaken first in a disposition of pliant surrender, and continued in a spirit of conquest, the pursuit of Christ in the world culminates logically in an impassioned enfolding, heavy with sorrow, in the arms of the cross. Eagerly and whole-heartedly, the soul has offered and surrendered itself to all the great currents of nature. When it reaches the term of all that it has gone through and when at long last it can see things with a mature eye, it realizes that no work is more effective or brings greater peace than to gather together, in order to soothe it and offer it to God, the suffering of the world; no attitude allows the soul to expand more freely, than to open itself, generously and tenderly – with and in Christ – *to sympathy with all suffering, to 'cosmic compassion'*.

Nieuport, 24 March 1916

– from *Writings in Time of War*, translated by René Hague, pp. 67–8.

WHAT fascinates me in life is being able to collaborate in a task, a reality, more durable than myself: it's in that spirit and with that in mind that I try to perfect myself and acquire a little more mastery over things. If death attacks me, it leaves untouched these causes, and ideas and realities, more solid and precious than myself; moreover, faith in Providence makes me believe that this death comes at its appointed hour, with its mysterious and special fruitfulness (not only for the soul's supernatural destiny, but also for the later progress of the earth). Why, then, should I be afraid and grieved, if the essential core of my life is left untouched – if the same design is still carried on, with no break or ruinous discontinuity? ... What I am apprehensive of in death is (why shouldn't I admit it?), besides the suffering, fear of the unknown, of a change of world (or at any rate a change in the outward aspect of the world). As you say, which comes to the same thing, the realities of faith are not felt with the same solidity as the reality of experience ... And so inevitably, providentially, there must be terror and bewilderment when one has to pass from one to the other. That, however, is just the moment to achieve the triumph of adoration, and of trust, and of the joy of forming part of a whole greater than oneself. I think that if anything can assuage the bitterness of death, it is still, and always will be, the practice (properly understood) of the passive attitude I have often urged on you. I don't mean that through death we shall return to the great current in which all things are absorbed, as the pantheist view of happiness envisages; yet at the same time we are caught up again, invaded, dominated, by the divine power – contained within the forces that disturb the most intimate depths of our organic being, those which are present above all in the irresistible urge that will lead our disembodied soul along the further paths that await it (as inevitably as the sun causes vapour to rise from the water on which its rays fall) . . . Death surrenders us totally to God; it makes us enter into him; we must, in return, surrender ourselves to death with absolute love and self-abandonment –

since, when death comes, all we can do is to surrender ourselves completely to the domination and guidance of God. Even as I write this, my thought is feeling its way; that's why it finds difficulty in expressing itself and appears trite or muddled. All the same, I feel that there'd be something to say about the joy (the healthy joy) of death, about its harmony in life, about the intimate connection (and at the same time the barrier) between the world of the dead and the world of the living, about the unity of both in one and the same cosmos. Death has been treated too much as a subject for melancholy reflection, or as an occasion for self-discipline, or as a rather hazy theological entity... What we have to do is to see it in its true context, see it as an active reality, as one more phase, in a world and a 'becoming' that are those of our own experience.

Ménil-sur-Saulx, 13 November 1916

— from *The Making of a Mind*, translated by René Hague, pp. 144–6.

AND I've come to think that the only, the supreme, prayer we can offer up, during these hours when the road before us is shrouded in darkness, is that of our Master on the cross: '*In manus tuas commendo spiritum meum.*' To the hands that broke and gave life to the bread, that blessed and caressed, that were pierced; ... to the kindly and mighty hands that reach down to the very marrow of the soul – that mould and create – to the hands through which so great a love is transmitted – it is to these that it is good to surrender our soul, above all when we suffer or are afraid. And in so doing there is a great happiness and great merit.

Ménil-sur-Saulx, 23 November 1916

– from *The Making of a Mind*, pp. 147–8.

By no means the least disturbing aspect of the problem of evil is this powerlessness of the world to develop successfully, I won't say the best, but at any rate a good part of itself... When you're confronted with this mystery, it's a good thing, as you so well said, to abandon yourself to the masterful current, as divine when it cancels out our efforts as when it carries us forward. After all, what really matters is surely to be united with God, and to fall in with the movements he imposes on us, whatever they may be. And is it not as beatifying to feel the influence of him we love exert itself to make us less (as his wisdom plans) rather than greater? – to go back to Blondel's words that you copied for me, 'the action of others on ourselves' is more clearly seen in sorrow than in enjoyment, and the same is thus true of the resulting joy.

Bagneux, 29 January 1917

– from *The Making of a Mind*, p. 176.

I MUST say that you analyse the pain of forgetting those one loves very justly and with great insight. There's a whole category of strangely distressing feelings that I'm only beginning to define at all accurately myself, and the one you describe is among them: those that tear the soul apart by opposing its most vital determinisms to its most vital affections. Have you sometimes experienced what it is to be unable to love people by whom you're loved most touchingly and whom you want with all your power to love (you know well enough that I'm not referring to you here)? It's happened to me – and I know no more exquisite pain. Then indeed is the soul sundered and torn by the action of the very forces that make it to be what it is and which are now seen to be endowed with a mysterious complexity – you are now experiencing, in relation to my uncle, a similar anguish: you are fighting against yourself. The true remedy, as you point out, is to turn your eyes towards our Lord, the centre of souls, and then, in a spirit of adoration, to bow before this inexorable law of Providence. What a domain, incidentally, there would be to explore, following up this problem of 'the soul in opposition to itself', for the psychologist or the novelist who could find his way in these dim regions.

Marne, 5 February 1917

– from *The Making of a Mind*, p. 180.

THE testing time had come.

But it did not bring the unalleviated sorrow I had expected, of being pulled up short by the uncertainties and limitations of every single particular good. On the contrary, a glorious, unsuspected joy invaded my soul. And why was this, Lord, if not because, in the collapse of those immediate supports I came so dangerously close to accepting for my life, I knew with a unique experiential certainty that I would never again rely for support on anything save your own divine consistence?

The power to appreciate and to open the heart is indispensable to the awakening and the maintenance of the mystical appetite. But *all the raptures they bring put together are not so effective as the icy chill of a disappointment* in showing us that you alone, my God, are stable. It is through sorrow, and not through joy, that your Godhead gradually assumes, *in our sentient faculty*, the higher reality it possesses in the nature of things, but which it is so difficult even for those who are most fully initiated to put into words.

That is why, if some day – if not before, it will at least be on the day I die – everything should begin to fall away from me, if some total catastrophe should tear down the structure, based on all the things I have sought for and loved, which makes up my life's work – then, when I see the naked form of your consistence rising up alone from the ruins, I believe that, with the help of your grace, Lord, the words that come to my lips will be the old paean of the ancient world, *Io triumpe!*

Beaulieu-les-Fontaines, Oise, 13 August 1917

– from *Writings in Time of War*, pp. 126–7.

WHAT is there in suffering that commits me so deeply to you?

Why, when you stretched out nets to imprison me, should I have thrilled with greater joy than when you offered me wings?

It is because the only element I hanker after in your gifts is the fragrance of your power over me and the touch of your hand upon me. For what exhilarates us human creatures more than freedom, more than the glory of achievement, is the joy of finding and surrendering to a beauty greater than man, the rapture of being possessed. So long as my movement and growth are dictated by my own desires, I can believe that I am my own master. But I do not feel your active influence so long as I follow its guidance. My ship seems to sail without rudder or sails. Yet when there comes a sudden squall of wind, when her way is suddenly checked, when she lies over on her beam-ends, then I feel the full strength of the force that holds me up. It is only in opposition to my own appetites, and only by conquering them, that your power, my God, takes on for my heart its complete reality, and stamps me to the quick with the beatifying imprint of its domination.

Blessed, then, be the disappointments which snatch the cup from our lips; blessed be the chains that force us to go where we would not.

Blessed be relentless time and the unending thraldom in which it holds us: the inexorable bondage of time that goes too slowly and frets our impatience, of time that goes too quickly and ages us, of time that never stops and never returns.

Blessed, above all, be death and the horror of falling back into the cosmic forces. At the moment of its coming a power as strong as the universe pounces upon our bodies to grind them to dust and dissolve them, and an attraction more tremendous than any material tension draws our unresisting souls towards their proper centre. Death causes us to lose our footing completely in ourselves so as to deliver us over to the powers of heaven and earth. This is its final terror – but it is also, for the mystic, the climax of his bliss: it is our final entry, there to remain for ever, into the milieu that dominates, that carries us off, that consumes.

'*Io triumpe.*'

Beaulieu-les-Fontaines, Oise, 13 August 1917

– from *Writings in Time of War*, pp. 131–2.

MORALITY is generally regarded as a system of actions and relationships that are *biologically secondary*, less immediate and less physical than material or vital relationships. This is a great mistake. One has only to study, from the point of view of 'creative union', its role in the evolution of living beings in order to see how profound is the morphogenic power of the Good. Through its two fundamental virtues of chastity and charity, practised in renunciation, the Christian moral system is strictly ordered towards the progressive unification of the living being.

By fighting against the powers in the being that cause it to disintegrate, *chastity* maintains the elements of Spirit in their state of hard-won coherence, and carries them further. *It unifies the monad in its own self.*

Conversely, *charity* is the force that stops beings from shutting themselves up in a self-centred folding-in of their energies, and makes them 'unbutton', open themselves and surrender themselves to one another: it makes them *find a centre outside themselves* and so enhance a higher centre of association. *It unifies the monads among one another*, a role that is particularly godlike and providential in a world in which the appearance of intelligence inaugurated a crisis of autonomy and individualism.

November 1917

– from *Writings in Time of War*, pp. 172–3.

THE only true death, the only good death, is a culminating outburst of life: it is the fruit of a desperate effort made by the living to become more pure, more stripped and bare, more taut as they force their way out of the zone in which they are imprisoned.

Vertus, 15 January 1918

– from 'La Grande Monade', in *Ecrits du Temps de la Guerre*, p. 246, translated by René Hague.

THE lack of satisfaction I find in nature – to the point where it causes me physical suffering – is chiefly the inevitable *superficiality* of our experience of it here below. Anything *new* we can contrive to discover or extract is contained within a zone limited beforehand by our faculties. As soon as we reach a certain depth, we're down to rock: we're ringed in by a barrier that we can't break through, that can only be broken through by some *complete organic transformation* such as death alone can bring about. Nature makes us want to die, so that we may see what lies within her (to die by the death which is the *term* of life brought by Providence *to its maturity*, one should add, if one is to follow the direction given by sound reasoning and experience): there, it seems to me, you have the final development of the emotion aroused when you look at things. Somewhat to my surprise, I found this view expressed by Baudelaire, somewhere in the *Fleurs du Mal* (a little corrupted by dilettantism and pessimism, of course): *To die, so that one may at last find one's way to something new.*

Vauciennes, 12 July 1918

– from *The Making of a Mind*, p. 214.

In brief, I was in no serious danger this time, and did nothing outstanding. That's probably why I was more vividly aware of the 'shadow of death', and the formidable gift that existence presents us with: an inevitable advance towards an inevitable, sentient end – a situation from which one can emerge only through physical dissolution . . . I believe I've never felt that to be so real . . . And then I understood a little better the agony of our Lord, on Good Friday. And the remedy seemed clearer to me, always the same: to abandon oneself with faith and love, to the divine future (the becoming) which is '*the* most real' of all, '*the* most living' – whose most terrifying aspect is that of being the most renewing (and hence the most creative, the most precious of all).

Carlepont, 28 August 1918

– from *The Making of a Mind*, pp. 230–1.

TRUST in God (and in the being which is maintained by him) does not, then, do away with death: but it makes death such that it opens the way to greater fullness of life... the greater the faith with which one allows death to carry one off, the more will death introduce one to some individually heightened form of existence...

Moyvillers, 12 September 1918

— from *The Making of a Mind*, pp. 235–6.

SICKNESS and error spell ruin to the small-minded, but the Christian, *if he has faith*, can make them enter into a combination from which *his* universe emerges with more sanctifying power in it and more of the divine. The Christian can make his own what is deadly poison to others, and assimilate it in such a way as to draw from it a new draught of life.

We must, in view of the practical uncertainty of the morrow, have thrown ourselves, in a true act of interior surrender, upon Providence as our sole support – Providence accepted as being as physically real as the objects of our disquietude; we must, in our suffering of the ills we have incurred, our remorse for the sins we have committed, our vexation over the opportunities we have missed, have forced ourselves to believe *unhesitatingly* that God is powerful enough to turn each and *every* particular evil into good; we must, despite some appearances to the contrary, have acted *without reservation* as though our being could make progress only when directed towards chastity, humility, loving-kindness.

We must, in the shadow of death, have forced ourselves not to look back to the past, but to seek in utter darkness the dawn of God.

Chavannes-sur-l'Etang, 28 September 1918

– from *Writings in Time of War*, pp. 241–2, 247.

HENCEFORTH, working upon a solid natural basis, upon a vigorous natural capacity for growth and self-forgetfulness, Christ's activity (with suffering as its most important instrument) will take the form of *substituting Christ* for the soul (of 'ecstasizing' the soul). The time has come for the creature who is dominated by Christ when '*Oportet illum crescere, me autem minui*', when 'he must grow greater, while I grow less'. This is the hour of the *specifically Christian* operation, when Christ, while preserving in man the treasures of human nature, empties him of his egocentrism and takes his heart – it is a grievous hour for our lower nature, abandoned to those *forces* in the world *that bring diminishment,* but one full of delight for the man who has the light of faith and feels that he is being driven out of himself and that he is dying, under the compelling power of a Communion.

Strasbourg, 22 December 1918

— from *Writings in Time of War*, p. 261.

All the same, I've been struck by the insistence with which the Church constantly repeats the final refrain *'Christus factus est obediens usque ad mortem crucis'*. That's obviously the exact and profound significance of the cross: obedience, submission to the law of life. To work patiently until death – and to accept everything, in a spirit of love, including death: there you have the essence of Christianity. Believe me, you should cast away all vain regret for the past and all vague anxiety for the future. Concentrate on obedience to God as, day by day, his will becomes manifest.

Paris, Good Friday (20 April) 1919

– from *The Making of a Mind*, p. 293.

I UNDERSTAND your anxiety about not being up to the level of your task. This is one of the great human problems. You have to face this problem squarely, in God's truth and light – given that we live under this sun. Don't get lost in vain inner self-examination about your capacities and value. But tell yourself, categorically, that, for the success of the enormous work of creation, God only needs one thing: that you should *do your best*. As soon as you give what you are capable of giving, you are united *in maximum measure* to the creative act; you couldn't be a more useful servant. You must grasp this crucial point: only one thing matters in life (in order that it may be fulfilled) and that is to keep exactly to the place, willed by God, that is indicated at every moment by the equilibrium established between our effort (to succeed, and develop ourselves) and the resistance of things (which limit us). So long as we are in this place we are a faithful and supremely useful atom in the universe, truly annexed to the body and heart of Christ. And don't forget that if we lack power over our inspiration and intelligence, we have in addition the resource of intensifying our intention and our faith. The longer I plod on, the more I realize that on [that] side our power is prodigious. The weaker and less confident you feel in yourself, the more you need to strengthen in yourself the vision of the omnipresent Being to whom you have vowed your effort. The humblest effort, accomplished in this loving awareness of acting (physically) *in Christo*, has reverberations (and this is fundamental to the Christian's faith) on the real fibres of the world that no purely 'human' shock could ever produce. All this amounts to saying: make good the deficiencies you feel by redoubling your inner life, your 'mystical vision'.

Tientsin, 12 December 1923

– from *Letters to Léontine Zanta*, translated by Bernard Wall, pp. 60–1.

LET us try to gather together in one single ocean the whole mass of passions, of anticipations, of fears, of sufferings, of happiness, of which each man represents one drop. It was into this vast sea that Christ plunged, so as to absorb it, through all his pores, in his entire person. It was this storm-tossed sea that he diverted into his mighty heart, there to make its waves and tides subject to the rhythm of his own life. That is the meaning of the ardent life of Christ, Christ the source of all our good, of Christ as he prays; and therein lies the unfathomable secret of his agony, and the incomparable virtue, too, of his death on the cross.

In itself, death is a failure and a stumbling-block. It is the blind revenge taken by the insufficiently mastered elements on the soul that hampers their autonomy. It comes into the world as the direst of weaknesses, the most bitter of our enemies. Nevertheless, in spite of this initial taint, it can be put to good use, and in an unexpected direction, by the processes of creative union. For a being to die, normally means to sink back into the Multiple; but it can also be for it the reshaping that is indispensable to its entry under the dominion of a higher soul. The bread we eat appears to be decomposed within us, but it nevertheless becomes our flesh. Could there not also be dissociations in the course of which the elements would never cease to be dominated by a unity that breaks them up only to give them a new form? . . .

In order that physiological death (the remains, in us, of the domination of the Multiple) could be transformed into a means of union, it was necessary – physically necessary – for the monads doomed to suffer death to learn to accept it with humility and love, and above all with immense trust. We had, intellectually and vitally, to overcome the horror with which destruction fills us. By subjecting himself to the trial of individual death, by his blessed acceptance of the death of the world, Christ effected this reversal of our outlook and fears. He vanquished death. He gave it, physically, the value of a metamorphosis – through which the world, with him, entered into God.

Tientsin, 25 March 1924

– from *Science and Christ*, translated by René Hague, pp. 62–3.

Death through action

THE vital logic of action is such that we cannot conquer our own selves and increase our stature except through a gradual death of ourselves. To act worthily and usefully, we have seen, is to achieve unity. But to be united is to be transformed into a greater than oneself. Ultimately, then, to act is to leave behind the material, the immediate, the self-centred, and so advance into the universal Reality that is coming to birth. All that rather involved way of putting it is simply a way of expressing the most commonplace and frequently met experience of our lives – the painfulness of hard work.

Nothing is more excruciating than effort, and that is true of spiritual effort too. If you ask the masters of the ascetical life what is the first, the most certain, and the most sublime of mortifications, they will all give you the same answer: it is the work of interior development by which we tear ourselves away from ourselves, leave ourselves behind, emerge from ourselves. Every individual life, if lived loyally, is strewn with the outer shells discarded by our successive metamorphoses – and the entire universe leaves behind it a long series of states in which it might well have been pleased to linger with delight, but from which it has continually been torn away by the inexorable necessity to grow greater. This ascent in a continual sloughing off of the old is indeed a way of the cross.

Tientsin, 25 March 1924

– from *Science and Christ*, p. 69.

Death through passivity

HERE we must be most careful to distinguish the two phases in the implementing, in the world around us, of the will of God: in other words, in the animation of secondary causes by the influx of the universal Christ. In itself, and directly, our bondage to the world – particularly those forms of it that irk us, that diminish us, that kill us – is not divine, nor is it in any way willed by God. It represents that portion of incompleteness and disorder which mars a creation that is still imperfectly unified. In so far as they are such, these forms of bondage are displeasing to God: and, in a first stage, God fights with us (and in us) against them. One day he will triumph; but, because the duration of our individual lives is out of all proportion to the slow evolution of the total Christ, it is inevitable that we shall never, during our time on earth, see the final victory. Almost every moment brings another check to our effort to grow, undermines it – and sooner or later we shall all experience decline and death. Christ, nevertheless, can never be overcome. If, then, we ask how the almighty power, which is his in virtue of his cosmic function, of saving and beatifying the elements of his Body in growth, will in some way re-establish itself, the answer is that it will do so by a remarkable *transformation*. The Incarnate Word masters the limitations and diminishments that the general progress of the cosmos does not allow him to remove (in the same way as a skilful sculptor masters the shortcomings of his marble), by integrating them (though without changing them) in a higher spiritualization of our beings. That is why, when we have fought to the bitter end to develop ourselves and win through, and find ourselves halted, beaten, by the forces of this world, then, *if we believe*, the power with which we clash so agonizingly suddenly ceases to be a blind or evil energy. Hostile matter vanishes. And, in its place, we find the divine Master of the world who 'under the species and appearance' of each and every event, moulds us, empties us of our self-love, and penetrates into us...

Sometimes Christ makes our sorrows and mishaps serve to direct us along loftier paths, in which we improve ourselves *by experience*: think of all the saints who became saints through having been worsted in some terrestrial field; but often, again, our losses and our failures do not seem to be compensated by any appreciable advantage, even spiritual. It is then, most of all, that we must hold firm to our trust in God. The world can attain God, in Christ Jesus, only by a complete recasting in which it must *appear* to be entirely lost, with *nothing* (of the terrestrial order) *that our experience could recognize as compensation*. When such a death, whether it be slow or rapid, takes place in us, we must open our hearts wide to the hope of union: never, if we so will it, will the animating power of the world have mastered us so fully.

Tientsin, 25 March 1924

– from *Science and Christ*, pp. 71–3.

My whole interior life is directed and confirmed more and more in union with God as found in 'all the inner and outer forces of this world'. But if this attitude is to be effective, *nothing* in these forces must be excluded; neither death nor 'persecution' in the field of ideas. If we believe, everything can be transformed into our Lord.

Linn-Si (Eastern Mongolia), 20 May 1924

– from *Letters to Léontine Zanta*, p. 67.

THE death of egoism is to understand that one is an element in a universe that personalizes itself (if I may venture to say so) by uniting itself with God (I do not say, by becoming God). So it is no longer oneself that one loves in oneself.

Peking, 13 June 1926

– from *Letters to Two Friends, 1926–1952*, translated by Helen Weaver, p. 33.

WE have to absorb evil in an excess of trust and faith.

Tientsin, 24 January 1927

- from letter to Edouard Le Roy (unpublished), translated by René Hague.

But in our present universe, as is all too clear, nothing can absolutely resist, but everything must sooner or later yield to the forces of death. Your love of life is a healthy and magnificent power; and you must jealously guard this spirit of resistance to physical diminution which helps you to bear suffering. But there is still something missing in your attitude: you do not yet sufficiently love *all* of life, *all* of the universe to agree, once the inevitable moment has come, to diminish (in appearance) and to pass lovingly into it. We must struggle against death with all our force, for it is our fundamental duty as living creatures. But when, by virtue of a state of things (transitory, no doubt, but inevitably linked to the state of growth of the world), death takes us, we must experience that paroxysm of faith in life that causes us to abandon ourselves to death as to a falling into a greater life. To love life so much, and to trust it so completely, that we embrace it and throw ourselves into it even in death – this is the only attitude that can calm and fortify you: to love extravagantly what is *greater than oneself*. Every union, especially with a greater power, involves a kind of death of the self. Death is acceptable only if it represents the physically necessary passage toward a union, the condition of a metamorphosis.

Marseille, 2 October 1927

– from *Letters to Two Friends, 1926–1952*, pp. 78–9.

THE moment has come to plumb the decidedly negative side of our existences – the side on which, however far we search, we cannot discern any happy result or any solid conclusion to what happens to us. It is easy enough to understand that God can be grasped in and through every life. But can God also be found in and through every death? This is what perplexes us deeply. And yet this is what we must learn to acknowledge as a matter of settled habit and practice, unless we abandon all that is most characteristically Christian in the Christian outlook; and unless we are prepared to forfeit commerce with God in one of the most widespread and at the same time most profoundly passive and receptive experiences of human life.

The forces of diminishment are our real passivities. Their number is vast, their forms infinitely varied, their influence constant. In order to clarify our ideas and direct our meditation we will divide them into two groups corresponding to the two forms under which we considered the forces of growth: the diminishments whose origin lies *within us*, and the diminishments whose origin lies *outside us*.

The external passivities of diminishment are all our bits of ill fortune. We have only to look back on our lives to see them springing up on all sides: the barrier which blocks our way, the wall that hems us in, the stone which throws us from our path, the obstacle that breaks us, the invisible microbe that kills the body, the little word that infects the mind, all the incidents and accidents of varying importance and varying kinds, the tragic interferences (upsets, shocks, severances, deaths) which come between the world of 'other' things and the world that radiates out from us. And yet when hail, fire and thieves had taken everything from Job – all his wealth and all his family – Satan could say to God: 'Skin for skin, and all that a man hath he will give for his life. But put forth thy hand, and touch his bone and his flesh: and then thou shalt see that he will curse thee to thy face.' In a sense the loss of things means little to us because we can always imagine getting them back. What is terrible for us is to be cut off from things through some inward diminishment that can never be retrieved.

Humanly speaking, the internal passivities of diminishment form the darkest element and the most despairingly useless years of our life. Some were waiting to pounce on us as we first awoke: natural failings, physical defects, intellectual or moral weaknesses, as a result of which the field of our activities, of our enjoyment, of our vision, has been pitilessly limited since birth. Others were lying in wait for us later on and appeared as suddenly and brutally as an accident, or as stealthily as an illness. All of us one day or another will come to realize, if we have not already done so, that one or other of these sources of disintegration has lodged itself in the very heart of our lives. Sometimes it is the cells of the body that rebel or become diseased; at other times the very elements of our personality seem to be in conflict or to detach themselves from any sort of order. And then we impotently stand by and watch collapse, rebellion and inner tyranny, and no friendly influence can come to our help. And if by chance we escape, to a greater or lesser extent, the critical forms of these assaults from without which appear deep within us and irresistibly destroy the strength, the light and the love by which we live, there still remains that slow, essential deterioration which we cannot escape: old age little by little robbing us of ourselves and pushing us on towards the end. Time, which postpones possession, time which tears us away from enjoyment, time which condemns us all to death – what a formidable passivity is the passage of time...

In death, as in an ocean, all our slow or swift diminishments flow out and merge. Death is the sum and consummation of all our diminishments: it is *evil* itself – purely physical evil, in so far as it results organically in the manifold structure of that physical nature in which we are immersed – but a moral evil too, in so far as in the society to which we belong, or in ourselves, the wrong use of our freedom, by spreading disorder, converts this manifold complexity of our nature into the source of all evil and all corruption.

We must overcome death by finding God in it. And by the same token, we shall find the divine established in our innermost hearts, in the last stronghold which might have seemed able to escape his reach.

... Christ has conquered death, not only by suppressing its evil effects, but by reversing its sting. By virtue of Christ's rising again, nothing any longer kills inevitably but everything is capable of becoming the blessed touch of the divine hands, the blessed influence of the will of God upon our lives. However marred by our faults, or however desperate in its circumstances, our position may be, we can, by a total re-ordering, completely correct the world that surrounds us, and resume our lives in a favourable sense. '*Diligentibus Deum omnia convertuntur in bonum.*' That is the fact which dominates all explanation and all discussion...

Let us ask ourselves how, and in what circumstances, our apparent deaths, that is to say the waste matter of our existences, can find their necessary place in the establishment, around us, of the kingdom of God and the *milieu* of God. It will help us to do this if we thoughtfully distinguish two phases, two periods, in the process which culminates in the transfiguration of our diminishments. The first of these phases is that of our struggle against evil. The second is that of defeat and of its transfiguration.

Tientsin, November 1926–March 1927

– from *Le Milieu Divin (The Divine Milieu)*, translated by Bernard Wall, pp. 59–62 (52–5).

When a Christian suffers, he says, 'God has touched me.' The words are pre-eminently true, though their simplicity summarizes a very complex series of spiritual operations; and it is *only when we have gone right through that whole series of operations* that we have the right to speak those words. For if, in the course of our encounters with evil, we try to distinguish what the schoolmen term 'the instants of nature', we shall have, on the contrary, to begin by saying, 'God wants to free me from this diminishment – God wants me to help him to take this cup from me.' To struggle against evil, and to reduce to a minimum even the ordinary physical evil which threatens us, is unquestionably the first act of our Father who is in heaven; it would be impossible to conceive him in any other way, and still more impossible to love him.

It is a perfectly correct view of things – and strictly consonant with the Gospel – to regard Providence across the ages as brooding over the world in ceaseless effort to spare that world its bitter wounds and to bind up its hurts. Most certainly it is God himself who, in the course of the centuries, awakens the great benefactors of humankind, and the great physicians, in ways that agree with the general rhythm of progress. He it is who inspires, even among those furthest from acknowledging his existence, the quest for every means of comfort and every means of healing. Do not men acknowledge by instinct this divine presence when hatreds are quenched and their protesting uncertainty resolved as they kneel to thank each one of those who have helped their body or their mind to freedom? Can there be any doubt of it? At the first approach of the diminishments we cannot hope to find God except by loathing what is coming upon us and doing our best to avoid it. The more we repel suffering at that moment, with our whole heart and our whole strength,* the more closely we cleave to the heart and action of God.

---

* Without bitterness and without revolt, of course, but with an *anticipatory tendency* to acceptance and final resignation. It is obviously difficult to separate the two 'instants of nature' without to some extent distorting them in describing them. But there is this to note: the necessity of the initial stage of resistance to evil is clear, and everyone admits it. The failure that follows on laziness, the illness contracted as a result of unjustified imprudence, could not be regarded by anyone as being the *immediate* will of God.

With God as our ally we are always certain of saving our souls. But we know too well that there is no guarantee that we shall always avoid suffering or even those inward defeats on account of which we can imagine our lives to ourselves as failures. In any event, all of us are growing old and all of us will die. This means to say that, however fine our resistance, at some moment or other we feel the constraining grip of the forces of diminishment, against which we were fighting, gradually gaining mastery over the forces of life, and dragging us, physically vanquished, to the ground. But how can we be defeated if God is fighting on our side? or what does this defeat mean?

The problem of evil, that is to say the reconciling of our failures, even the purely physical ones, with creative goodness and creative power, will always remain one of the most disturbing mysteries of the universe for both our hearts and our minds. A full understanding of the suffering of God's creatures (like that of the pains of the damned) presupposes in us an appreciation of the nature and value of 'participated being' which, for lack of any point of comparison, we cannot have. Yet this much we can see: on the one hand, the work which God has undertaken in uniting himself intimately to created beings presupposes in them a slow preparation in the course of which they (*who already exist, but are not yet complete*) cannot of their nature avoid the risks (increased by an original fault) involved in the imperfect ordering of the Multiple, in them and around them; and on the other hand, because the final victory of good over evil can only be completed in the *total* organization of the world, our infinitely short individual lives could not hope to know the joy, here below, of entry into the Promised Land. We are like soldiers who fall during the assault which leads to peace. God does not therefore suffer a preliminary defeat in our defeat because, although we appear to succumb individually, the world, in which we shall live again, triumphs in and through our deaths.

But this first aspect of his victory, which is enough to assure us of his omnipotence, is made complete by another disclosure – perhaps more direct and in every case more immediately experienceable by each of us – of his universal authority. In virtue of his very perfections,* God cannot ordain that the elements of a world in the course of growth – or at least of a fallen world in the process of rising again – should avoid shocks and diminishments, even moral ones: *'necessarium est ut scandala eveniant.'* But God will make it good – he will take his revenge, if one may use the expression – by making evil itself serve a higher good of his faithful, the very evil which the present state of creation does not allow him to suppress immediately. Like an artist who is able to make use of a fault or an

* Because his perfections cannot run counter to the nature of things, and because a world, assumed to be progressing towards perfection, or 'rising upward', is of its nature precisely still partially disorganized. A world without a trace or a threat of evil would be a world already consummated.

impurity in the stone he is sculpting or the bronze he is casting so as to produce more exquisite lines or a more beautiful tone, God, without sparing us the partial deaths, nor the final death, which form an essential part of our lives, transfigures them by integrating them in a better plan – *provided we lovingly trust in him*. Not only our unavoidable ills but our faults, even our most deliberate ones, can be embraced in that transformation, provided always we repent of them. Not everything is immediately good to those who seek God; but everything is capable of becoming good: '*omnia convertuntur in bonum.*'

What is the process and what are the phases by which God accomplishes this marvellous transformation of our deaths into a better life? Drawing on analogies from what we know how to bring about ourselves, and reflecting on the constant attitude and practical teaching of the Church with regard to human suffering, we may perhaps hazard an answer to this question.

It could be said that Providence, for those who believe in it, converts evil into good in three principal ways. Sometimes the check we have undergone will divert our activity on to objects, or towards a framework, that are more propitious – though still situated on the level of the human ends we are pursuing. That is what happened with Job, whose final happiness was greater than his first. At other times, more often perhaps, the loss which afflicts us will oblige us to turn for the satisfaction of our frustrated desires to less material fields, which neither worm nor rust can corrupt. The lives of the saints and, generally speaking, the lives of all those who have been outstanding for intelligence or goodness, are full of these instances in which one can see the man emerging ennobled, tempered and renewed from some ordeal, or even some downfall, which seemed bound to diminish or lay him low for ever. Failure in that case plays for us the part that the elevator plays for an aircraft or the pruning knife for a plant. It canalizes the sap of our inward life, disengages the purest 'components' of our being in such a way as to make us shoot up higher and straighter. The collapse, even when a moral one, is thus transformed into a success which, however spiritual it may be, is, nevertheless, felt *experientially.* In the presence of St Augustine, St Mary Magdalen or St Lydwine, no one hesitates to think *felix dolor* or *felix culpa.* With the result that, up to this point, we still 'understand' Providence.

But there are more difficult cases (the most common ones, in fact) where human wisdom is altogether out of its depth. At every moment we see diminishment, both in us and around us, which does not seem to be compensated by advantages on any perceptible plane: premature deaths, stupid accidents, weaknesses affecting the highest reaches of our being. Under blows such as these, man does not move upward in any direction that we can perceive; he disappears or remains grievously diminished. How can these diminishments which are altogether without compensation, wherein we see death at its most deathly, become for us a good? This is where we can see the third way in which Providence operates in the domain of our diminishments – the most effective way and the way which most surely makes us holy.

God, as we have seen, has already transfigured our sufferings by making them serve our conscious fulfilment. In his hands the forces of diminishment have perceptibly become the tool that cuts, carves and polishes within us the stone which is destined to occupy a definite place in the heavenly Jerusalem. But he will do still more, for, as a result of his omnipotence impinging upon our faith, events which show themselves experientially in our lives as pure loss will become an immediate factor in the union we dream of establishing with him.

Uniting oneself means, in every case, migrating, and dying partially in what one loves. But if, as we are sure, this being reduced to nothing in the other must be all the more complete the more we give our attachment to one who is greater than ourselves, then we can set no limits to the tearing up of roots that is involved on our journey into God. The progressive breaking down of our self-regard by the 'automatic' broadening of our human perspectives, when accompanied by the gradual spiritualization of our tastes and aspirations under the impact of certain setbacks, is no doubt a very real foretaste of that leap out of ourselves which must in the end deliver us from the bondage of ourselves into the service of the divine sovereignty. Yet the effect of this initial detachment is for the moment only to develop the centre of our personality to its utmost limits. Arrived at that ultimate point we may still have the impression of possessing ourselves in a supreme degree – of being freer and more active than ever. We have not yet crossed the critical point of our ex-centration, of our reversion to God. There is a further step to take: the one that makes us *lose all foothold within ourselves* – '*oportet illum crescere, me autem minui*'. We are still not lost to ourselves. What will be the agent of that definitive transformation? Nothing else than death.

In itself, death is an incurable weakness of corporeal beings, complicated, in our world, by the influence of an original fall. It is the sum and type of all the forces that diminish us, and against which we must fight without being able to hope for a personal, direct and immediate victory. Now the great victory of the Creator and Redeemer, in the Christian vision, is to have transformed what is in itself a universal power of diminishment and extinction into an essentially life-giving factor. God must, in some way or other, make room for himself, hollowing us out and emptying us, if he is finally to penetrate into us. And in order to assimilate us in him, he must break the molecules of our being so as to recast and remodel us. The function of death is to provide the necessary entrance into our inmost selves. It will make us undergo the required dissociation. It will put us into the state organically needed if the divine fire is to descend upon us. And in that way its fatal power to decompose and dissolve will be harnessed to the most sublime operations of life. What was by nature empty and void, a return to bits and pieces, can, in any human existence, become fullness and unity in God.

It was a joy to me, O God, in the midst of the struggle, to feel that in developing myself I was increasing the hold that you have upon me; it was a joy to me, too, under the inward thrust of life or amid the favourable play of events, to abandon myself to your Providence. Now that I have found the joy of utilizing all forms of growth to make you, or to let you, grow in me, grant that I may willingly consent to this last phase of communion in the course of which I shall possess you by diminishing in you.

After having perceived you as he who is 'a greater myself', grant, *when my hour comes*, that I may recognize you under the species of each alien or hostile force that seems bent upon destroying or uprooting me. When the signs of age begin to mark my body (and still more when they touch my mind); when the ill that is to diminish me or carry me off strikes from without or is born within me; when the painful moment comes in which I suddenly awaken to the fact that I am ill or growing old; and above all at that last moment when I feel I am losing hold of myself and am absolutely passive within the hands of the great unknown forces that have formed me; in all those dark moments, O God, grant that I may understand that it is you (provided only my faith is strong enough) who are painfully parting the fibres of my being in order to penetrate to the very marrow of my substance and bear me away within yourself.

The more deeply and incurably the evil is encrusted in my flesh, the more it will be you that I am harbouring – you as a loving, active principle of purification and detachment. The more the future opens before me like some dizzy abyss or dark tunnel, the more confident I may be – if I venture forward on the strength of your word – of losing myself and surrendering myself in you, of being assimilated by your body, Jesus.

You are the irresistible and vivifying force, O Lord, and because yours is the energy, because, of the two of us, you are infinitely the stronger, it is on you that falls the part of consuming me in the union that should weld us together. Vouchsafe, therefore, something more precious still than the grace for which all the faithful pray. It is not enough that I should die while communicating. Teach me *to treat my death as an act of communion.*

The above analysis (in which we have tried to distinguish the phases by which our diminishments may be divinized) has helped us to *validate to ourselves* the Christian formula, which is so comforting to those who suffer, 'God has touched me. God has taken away from me. His will be done.' As a result of this analysis we have understood how the two hands of God can reappear, more active and more penetrating than ever, beneath the evils that corrupt us from within, and the blows that break us up from without. But the analysis has a further result, almost as priceless as the first. It puts those of us who are Christians in a position to justify to those who are not Christians the legitimacy and the human value of resignation.

There are many reasonable men who honestly consider and denounce Christian resignation as being one of the most dangerous and soporific elements in 'the opium of the people'. Next to disgust with the earth, there is no attitude which the Gospel is so bitterly reproached with having fostered as that of passivity in the face of evil – a passivity which can go as far as a perverse cultivation of suffering and diminishment. As we have already said, with reference to 'false detachment': this accusation, or even suspicion, is infinitely more effective, at this moment, in preventing the conversion of the world than all the objections drawn from science or philosophy. A religion which is judged to be inferior to our human ideal – in spite of the marvels by which it is surrounded – is already *condemned*. It is therefore of supreme importance for the Christian to understand and live submission to the will of God in the *active* sense which, as we have said, is the only orthodox sense.

No, if he is to practise to the full the perfection of his Christianity, the Christian must not falter in his duty to resist evil. On the contrary, during the first phase, as we have seen, he must fight sincerely and with all his strength, in union with the creative force of the world, to drive back evil – so that nothing in him or around him may be diminished. During this initial phase, the believer is the convinced ally of all those who think that humanity will not succeed unless it strives with all its might to realize its potentialities. And as we said with reference to human development, the believer is more closely tied than anyone to this great task, because in his eyes the victory of humanity over the diminishments of the world – even physical and natural – to some extent conditions the fulfilment and consummation of the quite specific Reality which he adores. As long as resistance is possible, the son of heaven will resist too – as firmly as the most worldly children of the world – everything that deserves to be scattered or destroyed.

Should he meet with defeat – the personal defeat which no human being can hope to escape in his brief single combat with forces whose order of magnitude and evolution are universal – he will, like the conquered pagan hero, still inwardly resist. Though he is stifled and constrained, his efforts will still be sustained. At that point, however, he will see a new realm of possibilities open out before him, instead of having nothing to compensate for and master his coming death except the melancholy and questionable consolation of stoicism (which, if carefully analysed, would probably prove in the end to owe its beauty and consistency to a despairing faith *in the value of sacrifice*). This hostile force that lays him low and disintegrates him can become for him a loving principle of renewal, if he accepts it with faith while never ceasing to struggle against it. On the experiential plane, everything is lost. But in the realm of the supernatural, as it is called, *there is a further dimension* which allows God to achieve, *insensibly*, a mysterious reversal of evil into good. Leaving the zone of human successes and failures behind him, the Christian accedes by an effort of trust in the greater than himself to the region of supra-sensible transformations and growth. His resignation is no more than the thrust which lifts the field of his activity higher.

We have come a long way, Christianly speaking, from the justly criticized notion of 'submission to the will of God' which is in danger of weakening and softening the fine steel of the human will, brandished against all the powers of darkness and diminishment. We must understand this well, and cause it to be understood: to find and to do the will of God (even as we diminish and as we die) does not imply either a direct encounter or a passive attitude. I have no right to regard the evil that comes upon me through my own negligence or fault as being the touch of God.* I can only unite myself to the will of God (as endured passively) *when all my strength is spent*, at the point where my activity, fully extended and straining towards betterment (understood in ordinary human terms), finds itself continually counter-weighted by forces tending to halt me or overwhelm me. Unless I do everything I can to advance or resist, I shall not find myself at the *required point* – I shall not submit to God as much as I might have done or as much as he wishes. If, on the contrary, I persevere courageously, I shall rejoin God across evil, deeper down than evil; I shall draw close to

* Though the harm which results from my negligence can become the will of God for me on condition I repent and correct my lazy or indifferent attitude of mind. Everything can be taken up again and recast in God, even one's faults.

him; and at that moment the optimum of my 'communion in resignation' necessarily coincides (by definition) with the maximum of fidelity to the human task.

Tientsin, November 1926–March 1927

— from *Le Milieu Divin* (*The Divine Milieu*), pp. 62–73 (55–66).

ILLNESS naturally tends to give sufferers the feeling that they are useless or even a burden on the earth. Almost inevitably they feel as if cast up by the great stream of life, lying by sheer ill-luck incapable of work or activity. Their state seems to have no meaning. It reduces them, they might say, to inaction amidst a universe in action.

The following observations are designed to help dissipate these depressing views by showing, from a hypothetical standpoint, the place and use of suffering in the construction even of the visible world.

In the first place the world is under construction. This is a fundamental truth which must be understood at the start, and so thoroughly understood as to become habitual and more or less natural to our thought. At first sight, beings and their fate may possibly appear to be distributed by chance, or at least arbitrarily, over the face of the earth. We are within an ace of thinking that each one of us might have been born indifferently earlier or later, here or there, more or less fortunate. The universe from the beginning to the end of its history might seem like a sort of vast flower-bed in time and space in which the flowers are interchangeable at the gardener's whim. This view seems at fault. The more we reflect, making use of what we have learnt from science, philosophy and religion, each along its own lines, the more we see that the world must be compared not to a bundle of elements in artificial juxtaposition but to an organized system, informed by a broad unity of growth proper to itself. Through the centuries, a general plan appears truly to be in course of realization around us. Something is afoot in the universe, a result is working out which can best be compared to a gestation and birth: the birth of a spiritual reality formed by souls and the matter they draw after them. Laboriously, by way of human activity and thanks to it, the new earth is gathering, isolating and purifying itself. No, we are not like flowers in a bunch, but the leaves and flowers of a great tree, on which each appears at its time and place, according to the demands of the Whole.

This conception of a world in the state of growth might seem ingenious but abstract. In fact it has important practical consequences. For it leads to nothing less than the renewal in our minds of the idea we have ourselves formed either of the value of personal human effort (which increases with the whole work of the universe of which it is part) or (and it is only this that interests us here) of the value of individual human pain. Let us explain this last point a little, by returning to the comparison of the bunch of flowers and the tree.

In a bunch one would be surprised to see imperfect or 'sickly' flowers because the constituents have been gathered one by one, and artificially put together. On a tree, on the other hand, which has had to fight against inner accidents in its development and the external accidents of bad weather, broken branches, torn leaves, parched, sickly or wilted flowers are 'in place': they express the more or less difficult conditions of growth encountered by the trunk that bears them.

Similarly, in a universe where each creature forms a little whole enclosed and desired for its own sake and theoretically transposable at will, we should have some difficulty in mentally justifying the presence of individuals sadly arrested in their possibilities of ascent. Why this arbitrary inequality, these gratuitous restrictions? On the other hand, if the world in fact represents a work of achievement at present taking place; if at birth we are really thrown into the midst of a battle, we can see that, for the success of the universal effort of which we are at the same time the participators and the stake, it is inevitable that there shall be pain. The world, seen by experience at our level, is an immense groping, an immense search, an immense attack; its progress can take place only at the expense of many failures, of many wounds. Sufferers of whatever species are the expression of this stern but noble condition. They are not useless and dwarfed. They are simply paying for the forward march and triumph of all. They are casualties, fallen on the field of honour.

Let us go a little further. In the collective man formed by all men together and subordinated to Christ within the 'mystical body', there are, as St Paul has told us, different organs and functions. What part can we imagine to be more specially entrusted with the task of sublimating and spiritualizing the general work of progress and conquest? The contemplatives and prayerful, no doubt. But also, most certainly, the sick and suffering. By nature and temperament sufferers are in a sense driven out of themselves, compelled to depart from the prevailing forms of life. Are they not therefore by this very fact destined and chosen for the task of raising the world above immediate enjoyment towards an ever higher light? It is for them to stretch up to the divine more deliberately and more purely than the rest. It is for them to bring aid to their brothers who are working like miners in the bowels of matter. Thus it is those who bear in their weakened bodies the weight of the world in motion that, by providential compensation, prove the most active agents in the very progress that seems to be sacrificing and breaking them.

If these remarks are true, the sick man in his apparent inactivity has a very grand human task to fulfil. He must of course never cease to aim at his own cure and recovery. Also he must of course use all the strength that remains to him for the different kinds of sometimes extremely productive work that are within his powers. Christian resignation, in fact, is just the opposite of giving up. Once he has resolved to combat his sickness in this way, the sick man must realize that in proportion to his sickness he has a special function to perform, in which no one can replace him: the task of co-operating in the transformation (one might say conversion) of human suffering.

What a vast ocean of human suffering spreads over the entire earth at every moment! Of what is this mass formed? Of blackness, gaps and rejections? No, let me repeat, of potential energy. In suffering the world's upward force is concealed in a very intense form. The whole question is how to liberate it and give it a consciousness of its significance and potentialities. The world would leap high towards God if all the sick together were to turn their pain into a common desire that the kingdom of

God should come to rapid fruition through the conquest and organization of the earth. All the sufferers of the earth joining their sufferings so that the world's pain might become a great and unique act of consciousness, elevation and union. Would not this be one of the highest forms that the mysterious work of creation could take in our sight?

Could it not be precisely for this that the creation was completed in Christian eyes by the passion of Jesus? On the cross, we are perhaps in danger of seeing only an individual suffering, a single act of expiation. The creative power of that death escapes us. Let us take a broader glance, and we shall see that the cross is the symbol and place of an action whose intensity is beyond expression.

Even from the earthly point of view, the crucified Jesus, fully understood, is not rejected or conquered. It is, on the contrary, he who bears the weight and draws ever higher towards God the universal march of progress. Let us act like him, in order to be in our whole existence united with him.

1 April 1933

— from *Human Energy*, translated by J. M. Cohen, pp. 48–52.

We must, to a certain extent, look for a stable port; but if life keeps tearing us away, not letting us settle anywhere, this in itself may be a call and a benediction. The world is understood and will be saved, as I have already written to you, only by those who have no place to lay their heads. Personally, I ask God to let me die (metaphorically, at least) by the side of the road.

Paris, 13 September 1935

— from *Letters to Two Friends, 1926–1952*, p. 88.

If everything in us and around us is indeed moving towards a great union by love, the world should seemingly be bathed in joy. How is it that, on the contrary, it is falling more deeply into grief? Why all these tears and blood? How can suffering enter into a personal universe?

My answer to this question, the most anguishing of all for the human mind, will be this: in the universe that I have discussed the problem of evil presents no special difficulty. In fact it finds the most satisfying theoretical solution, and even some indication of a practical one.

A world on the way to concentration of consciousness, you think, would be all joy? On the contrary, I answer. It is just such a world that is the most natural and necessary seat of suffering. Nothing is more beatific than union attained; nothing more laborious than the pursuit of union. For three reasons at least a personalizing evolution is necessarily painful: it is basically a plurality; it advances by differentiation; it leads to metamorphoses.

4 May 1936

– from *Human Energy*, pp. 84–5.

It can truly be said that real pain entered the world with man, when for the first time a reflective consciousness became capable of observing its own diminution. The only true *evil* is suffered by personality. In what form does death present itself in the personal universe that we have outlined here?

I will answer: as a metamorphosis.

We must return again to this important point on which we have already touched when considering the formation and consummation of the personality: no physical agent can grow indefinitely without reaching the phase of a change of state. For a more or less long period, things simply vary, without ceasing to remain recognizably themselves. And then at a given moment a complete reconstitution of the elements becomes necessary, so that it may be of a magnitude to enter a new realm of possible progress. The force of personalization, in which we believed we had recognized the mainspring of evolution, apparently meets with these discontinuities in the course of its development. On reaching a certain limit of concentration, the personal elements find themselves faced with a threshold to be crossed before they can enter the sphere of action of a centre of higher order. It is not only necessary for them at that moment to rouse themselves from the inertia which tends to immobilize them. The moment has come also for them to surrender to a transformation which appears to take from them all that they have already acquired. *They can grow no greater without changing*. Then comes the agony of losing ourselves in the monstrous mass of humanity that awaits us or the still greater agony of escaping by the swift or slow dissolution of the body from the totality of the framework of experience into which we were born.

Deaths, death, are no more than critical points scattered on the road of union.

Peking, 4 May 1936

– from *Human Energy*, pp. 87–8.

ACCEPT what has happened as you would receive the Host at Communion. When we have done our best, 'everything that happens calls for our worship'. That is the last word of human wisdom and of sanctity.

Peking, 9 May 1944

– from letter to Madame Henry Cosme (unpublished), translated by René Hague.

Do not *brace* yourself against suffering. Try to close your eyes and surrender yourself, as if to a great loving energy. This attitude is neither weak nor absurd, it is the only one that cannot lead us astray – unless life itself is inherently a contradictory and stupid thing, which its very existence belies. It is still too soon, no doubt, for you to recover: try to 'sleep', with that *active* sleep of confidence which is that of the seed in the fields in winter . . . As I've said before, this is the true and great prayer of moments of great sickness.

19 April 1948

— from *Letters to Two Friends, 1926–1952*, p. 104.

La Porte Etroite is a clever but extremely unpleasant book: this idea of a value of sacrifice and pain for the sake of sacrifice and pain itself (whereas the value of pain is simply to pay for some useful conquest!) is a dangerous (and very 'Protestant') perversion of the 'meaning of the cross' (the true meaning of the cross is: 'Toward progress through effort').

15 rue Monsieur, Paris, 18 September 1948

— from *Letters to Two Friends, 1926–1952*, p. 187.

To a perfectly clear-sighted observer who looked at the earth for a long time and from a great height, our planet would appear blue at first, from the oxygen that envelops it; then green, from the vegetation that covers it; and then luminous, and ever more luminous, from the thought intensifying on its surface; but also dark, and ever more dark, with a suffering that increases in quantity and sharpness in step with the rise of consciousness throughout the ages.

Think of the total suffering of the whole earth at each particular moment ... If only we were able to heap up this formidable magnitude, determine its volume, weigh it, count it, analyse it, what an astronomical mass it would be, what a terrifying total. And what a finely graduated spectrum of shades of painfulness, from physical torture to all forms of moral anguish. And if only, too, there were suddenly a conductivity between bodies and souls, so that all the pain and all the joy of the world flowed together, who can say on which side the balance would come to rest? . . .

Yes, the more Man becomes man, the more the problem of evil becomes engrained, and the heavier its burden – in his flesh, in his nervous system, in his mind – the problem of evil to be understood and of evil to be suffered.

A more correct outlook on the universe in which we are involved is now bringing us, it is true, the beginning of an answer to that problem. In the vast process of organization from which life emerges, we are coming to see, every success has necessarily to be paid for by a high percentage of failure. There is no progress in being without some mysterious tribute of tears, blood and sin. It is not to be wondered at, then, if, as we look around us, there are some shadows which grow deeper as the light grows stronger: for, when we look at it from this angle, suffering, in all its forms and all its degrees, is (at least partially) no more than the natural consequence of the very movement by which we ourselves are brought into being.

The evidence of universal experience is beginning to make us accept this complementary mechanism of good and evil, in an abstract way, intellectually. But if our hearts are to accommodate themselves to this stern law of creation, and not to rebel against it, it is psychologically essential that, in the painful wastage attaching to the operation by which we are formed, we find some further positive value, which will transfigure it and so make it acceptable to us.

And it is here we meet, fulfilling a function that nothing can replace, the astonishing Christian revelation of a suffering that can be transformed (provided it be *correctly* accepted) into an expression of love and a principle of union. Suffering treated first of all as an adversary to be conquered; suffering fought against with vigour to the bitter end; and yet, at the same time, suffering rationally and cordially accepted in as much as it wrenches us away from our concentration on self, counterbalances our faults, and so succeeds in super-centering us on God. Yes: suffering itself, obscure and ugly, elevated for the most humble patient into a supremely active principle of universal humanization and divinization – this is what the vast spiritual dynamic, born of the cross, becomes when it reaches its peak; and it is one concrete example of this, among countless similar cases, that the following pages are an attempt to describe.

With dazzling clarity we can see in the woman whose inner portrait Monique Givelet,* on behalf of the Union Catholique des Malades, draws for us here, the marks and the effects that characterize an authentically *good*

* President of the Union Catholique des Malades in 1949.

suffering. We see a constant refinement of the critical sense, and an ever better balanced appreciation of human values; an heroic determination to meet with a smile, until the very end, all that the sick have passively to accept; an increasing emotional sensitivity to the joys and sorrows of others; a clearness of sight that gives new strength and simplicity to all that is real, seen in the omnipresence of God. All these come together to form a unique attractive force, which brings peace and sheds the radiance of a halo.

An overplus of Spirit born from a deficiency of matter.

Here, indeed, we see the miracle, constantly renewed over two thousand years, of a possible Christification of suffering . . .

O Marguerite, my sister, while I, in my devotion to the positive forces of the universe, was roaming over continents and oceans, my whole being passionately taken up in watching the rise of all the earth's tints and shades, you, stretched out motionless on your bed of sickness, were silently transforming into light, deep within yourself, the most grievous shadows of the world.

Tell me, in the eyes of the Creator, which of us will have chosen the better part?

Paris, 8 January 1950

— from Teilhard de Chardin's preface to Marguerite-Marie Teilhard de Chardin's *L'Energie Spirituelle de la Souffrance*, pp. 9–12, translated by René Hague.